BIOGRAPHIC
ABBA

BIOGRAPHIC
ABBA

VIV CROOT

**ILLUSTRATED BY
MATT CARR**

AMMONITE
PRESS

The author would like to express her thanks to Geoff Davies
for his studio technique advice and musical information.

First published 2020 by
Ammonite Press
an imprint of Guild of Master Craftsman Publications Ltd
Castle Place, 166 High Street, Lewes, East Sussex, BN7 1XU,
United Kingdom
www.ammonitepress.com

ISBN 978 1 78145 408 4

A catalogue record for this book is available from the
British Library.

Publisher: Jason Hook
Concept Design: Matt Carr
Design & Illustration: Matt Carr & Robin Shields
Editor: Laura Paton

Colour reproduction by GMC Reprographics
Printed and bound in Turkey

CONTENTS

ICONOGRAPHIC

WHEN WE CAN RECOGNIZE A BAND BY
A SET OF ICONS, WE CAN ALSO RECOGNIZE
HOW COMPLETELY THOSE MUSICIANS
AND THEIR MUSIC HAVE ENTERED OUR
CULTURE AND OUR CONSCIOUSNESS.

INTRODUCTION

When ABBA burst onto the international scene in 1974, they made an instant impact: the eye-watering costumes, the glitter, the beaming smiles, the irresistible singalong tunes and that distinctive Scandinavian Wall of Sound. They were Sweden's own wholesome supergroup, four individually successful professionals with established but separate music careers in their homeland, and they came in pairs. They gave us almost a decade of euphoric hook-laden hits before first Björn and Agnetha, and then Benny and Anni-Frid, separated and divorced in quick succession. The glitter lost its sparkle; it was as if Cinders and Charming had decided to call it a day and send back the glass slipper. Officially, they were on a break; they just never came back from it. They'd had a dream, and we had all shared it, but it was, apparently, over.

Because ABBA had launched themselves from the platform of the terminally uncool Eurovision Song Contest, every self-respecting 'hip young gunslinging' music critic of the time mocked them mercilessly. Their music was considered easy, cheesy and, worst of all, pop. It was disposable. After their glory years, the fall from grace was instant. Throughout the rest of the 1980s they and their music were scorned, but one group of fans kept the faith: ABBA had always had a significant gay following, and they did not give up on the band. Björn, speaking in 2011, was convinced that the 1990s revival happened because the band had remained popular on the gay scene. Indeed, it was unabashed ABBA fan Andy Bell, from the synthpop duo Erasure, who helped to inspire their renaissance with Erasure's EP *ABBA-esque* (1992).

More support came from Australian tribute act Björn Again. They started out as a parody, but quickly realized the artless sophistication of ABBA's music and the uncynical enjoyment of their growing audiences. When *ABBA Gold* was released (also 1992), it sold by the truckload. Gradually it became okay to admit that you liked ABBA. Real musicians, rather than people who just critiqued music, came out in support of ABBA's sheer musical perfectionism. And they were cool musicians: Elvis Costello, Dave Grohl, Kurt Cobain, Pete Townshend, Glen Matlock, Ray Davies, Nile Rodgers, Björk, Brian May. Posturing about ABBA's naffness started to look silly.

So what makes ABBA's music abide? The seductive earworms and the singalong choruses lure you in, but what makes an ABBA song stick is something darker. It's what lies beneath. You can't judge a book by its cover, as Willie Dixon observed, even if that cover is an intricate surface full of hooks and twiddles and unlikely instrumental breaks (xylophone, accordion, marimba) on top of the multiple layerings, precision tuning and timing, ingenious use of space and volume and, flowing over it all, the crystalline shimmer of Agnetha and Anni-Frid, in harmony or unison or both.

"THEY WERE THE ONLY GROUP THAT SET MY SPINE TINGLING. THEY MADE GREAT POP TUNES THAT HAVE STOOD THE TEST OF TIME."

—Andy Bell, lead singer of Erasure, taken from *ABBA: The Book* by Jean-Marie Potiez, 2000

The critics had sneered that ABBA lacked that all-important shot of rhythm and blues, the black African-American tradition that is the basis of rock music. This is largely true, but what they have instead, and in abundance, is the deep existential melancholy of the north. Scandinavian countries know all about the darkness; it's built into their souls. They live, literally, with darkness at noon and the midnight sun. Norse mythology is the cultural expression of melancholic fatalism: life is a constant battle between light and dark, and come Ragnarök and the end of days the dark side will win and Ouroboros, the world serpent, will devour the Earth and us. There will be no reprieve. What else can you do but dance on the edge of the abyss?

And what better tune to do it to than ABBA's perfect pop masterwork 'Dancing Queen'? On the surface a joyous Dionysiac celebration, but actually an anthem for doomed youth. Listen to the lyrics. The singer isn't the dancing queen, they are an observer: "See that girl, watch that scene." Is it the singer's younger self? Is it a self they would like to have been? Is this nostalgia and regret for what was, what should have been, or what never was? Or is it a reminder that the time of their own life has been and gone and that there is only one end? ABBA smuggled the angel of death into the disco. No wonder heavy metal bands love them.

All ABBA's songs are shot through with melancholy, and they got darker as the band matured. Compare the exuberant yet anxious triumph of 'Waterloo' with the nuanced adult heartbreak of 'The Winner Takes it All'. ABBA's genius was to unite an immaculate pop sensibility with the existential melancholy of the human condition. And that gives meaning that everyone can grasp.

Now ABBA really are gold. Shifting over 380 million albums and singles, they are outsold only by The Beatles. In 2019, *Gold* passed its 90th week on the UK Official Albums Chart, making it the longest running Top 100 album ever. They are part of the cultural landscape; they even have a dedicated museum. *Mamma Mia!*, the stage musical and both films, has introduced new generations to their songs, and re-enchanted original fans. Most of their songs are now preserved forever in its simple yet universal story – maybe 'saga' would be a better word. There are still no plans for a comeback, unless as ABBA-tars – holograms of their younger selves – but maybe there is no need now, as they are not going away.

"IT IS BANAL SONGS SUCH AS THEIRS WHICH HELP FURTHER MANKIND'S UNDERSTANDING OF MANKIND. THE SONGS WERE BRILLIANTLY CONSTRUCTED. ABBA IS ART."

—Philip Hauenstein, music lecturer, taken from *ABBA: The Book* by Jean-Marie Potiez, 2000

ABBA

01
LIFE

A+B+B

→A=Au

"I'LL TELL YOU WHAT I TELL EVERYONE...
IF IT'S A FORMULA, WHY DON'T
YOU GO OUT AND FIND IT?"

—Stig Anderson,
Rolling Stone,
July 1977

ROOTS!

ABBA did not grow organically; they were not shaped by common landscape – geographically or culturally – nor even a shared era. Although they were all born within five years of the end of the Second World War, they underwent very different experiences. They were not childhood friends, neither did they go to college or work together, because they started out at different times and from different parts of Sweden – one of

ANNI-FRID (FRIDA) SYNNI LYNGSTAD

BORN:
15 November 1945 in Bjørkåsen, Norway

GÖRAN BROR BENNY ANDERSSON

BORN:
16 December 1946 in Stockholm, Sweden

BJÖRN KRISTIAN ULVAEUS

BORN:
25 April 1945 in Gothenburg, Sweden

STIG 'STIKKAN' ANDERSON

Born on 25 January 1931 in Hova, near Mariestad, in the Västergötland province of Sweden, manager and musician Stig was to blossom into the (mostly) benign Svengali who created ABBA and put them on the map.

MORE NORDIC NOISEMAKERS

THE CARDIGANS, one of Sweden's most internationally known rock bands, were formed in 1992 in Agnetha's home town of Jönköping.

YNGWIE MALMSTEEN, born in 1963 in Stockholm, Benny's home town, started his musical career in 1982 and went on to become one of the world's foremost heavy metal axemen.

ACE OF BASE were formed in 1990 in Gothenburg, Björn's home town; they became the third-highest selling Swedish band after ABBA and Roxette.

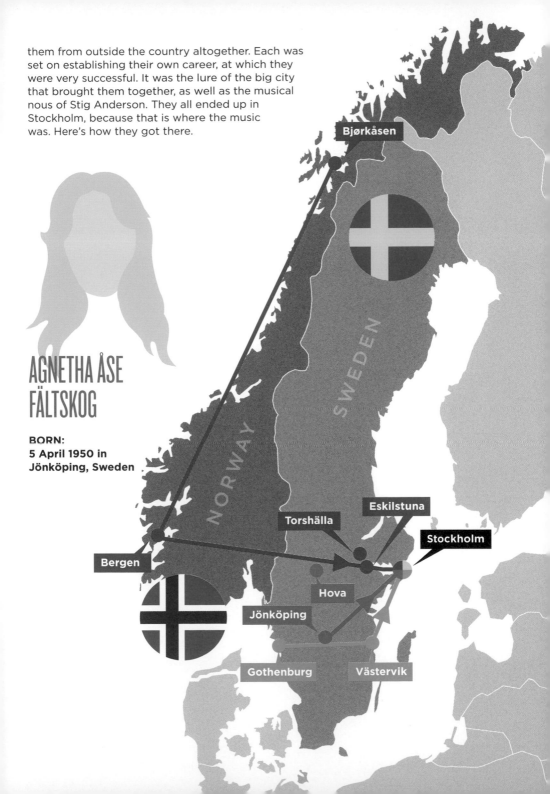

them from outside the country altogether. Each was set on establishing their own career, at which they were very successful. It was the lure of the big city that brought them together, as well as the musical nous of Stig Anderson. They all ended up in Stockholm, because that is where the music was. Here's how they got there.

AGNETHA ÅSE FÄLTSKOG

BORN:
5 April 1950 in
Jönköping, Sweden

Bjørkåsen

NORWAY

SWEDEN

Torshälla

Eskilstuna

Stockholm

Bergen

Hova

Jönköping

Gothenburg

Västervik

ANNI-FRID

Anni-Frid was the ABBA outsider, the contrasting element that stimulates creative tension, the one that experienced the devastation of war and came up early against the harsher side of life. She was born in Norway, a country at war, the illegitimate daughter of the enemy (her father was a German officer), and lost her mother when she was two. By the time she got to ABBA, she had been married and divorced, had two children, and had been singing and touring solo and with various bands for a decade.

INFLUENCES

NORWEGIAN FOLK MUSIC

JAZZ FROM BIG BAND ERA

PEGGY LEE

ELLA FITZGERALD

1 ALBUM RELEASED

13 SINGLES

DIVORCE

2 CHILDREN

Made all her own stage clothes

Won Swedish TV talent show, *New Faces*

Took part in song contests in Japan and Venezuela

AGNETHA

Although Agnetha was the youngest of the group – a small fierce blonde with a reported whim of iron – she was by far the best known and most successful. Born into a comfortable provincial family of keen amateur musicians and encouraged by her father, an enthusiastic amateur showman, she soon developed her natural musical talent. She was as interested in composition as singing. At 17, her first single, self-penned, went to number one; she came to ABBA already a rising star, with a bunch of solid hit singles and two albums to her name.

INFLUENCES

SWEDISH TRADITIONAL MUSIC

CONNIE FRANCIS

ARETHA FRANKLIN

MARIANNE FAITHFULL

2 ALBUMS RELEASED

17 SINGLES

15 TOP 10 HITS

BROKEN ENGAGEMENT

Formed three-piece girl band, The Cambers

NO. 1 HIT
'Jag var så Kär'

BJÖRN

Smart, self-contained and hardworking, Björn was the pragmatic frontman who didn't mind wearing trousers he could not sit down in if it brought success, but who sometimes had to remind himself to smile on stage. He taught himself guitar as a hobby (it didn't come easily – his family were not naturally musical) and was all set for a career in law or engineering when the music bug bit and he became the leading light of folk group, the West Bay Singers, who later became the Hootenanny Singers. By the time he came to ABBA, he was already a star as part of one of Sweden's top groups, a solo artist and one half of Björn & Benny.

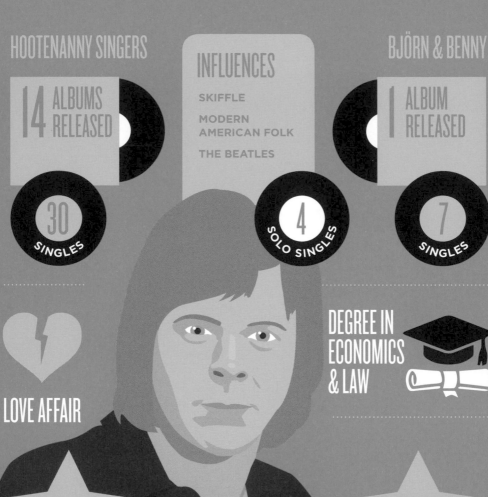

HOOTENANNY SINGERS

14 ALBUMS RELEASED

30 SINGLES

INFLUENCES

SKIFFLE

MODERN AMERICAN FOLK

THE BEATLES

4 SOLO SINGLES

BJÖRN & BENNY

1 ALBUM RELEASED

7 SINGLES

LOVE AFFAIR

DEGREE IN ECONOMICS & LAW

Member of Sweden's top folk group

West Bay Singers were named by his mother

BENNY

The cheese to Björn's chalk, Benny was the musical one. Unflappable and easy-going, Benny was one of nature's stoners, with no need for illegal substances. Born into a musical family, he played piano, accordion, harmonica – anything really – with intuitive ease, but never learnt how to read or write music. After leaving school at 15, he took dead-end jobs so that he could play the clubs at night. He drifted into early fatherhood and out again, stumbled into the Hep Stars (Sweden's hottest boy band) almost by accident, and met Björn, his future songwriting partner, completely by chance. By the time he got to ABBA, he had already backed himself into stardom.

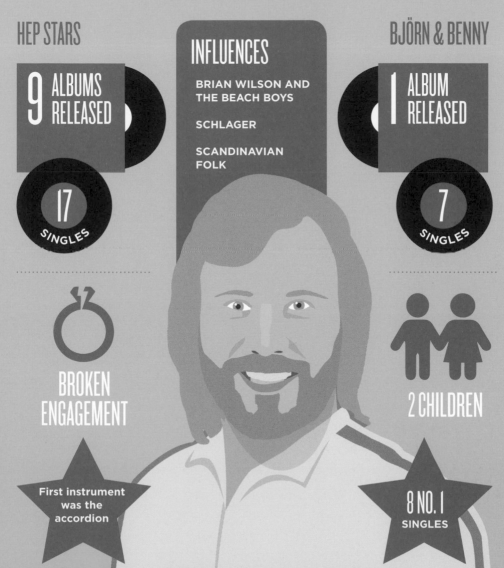

HEP STARS

9 ALBUMS RELEASED

17 SINGLES

INFLUENCES

BRIAN WILSON AND THE BEACH BOYS

SCHLAGER

SCANDINAVIAN FOLK

BJÖRN & BENNY

1 ALBUM RELEASED

7 SINGLES

BROKEN ENGAGEMENT

First instrument was the accordion

2 CHILDREN

8 NO. 1 SINGLES

THE NAME OF THE GAME

Through the Sixties, the workaholic Stig Anderson established a thriving music publishing business, while his future superstars chased their musical dreams with a good deal of success. Their creative and romantic paths began to criss-cross until they entwined, with Stig pulling the strings and bestowing upon them a name that would overshadow all of their early achievements.

ANNI-FRID
AGE 18 (IN 1963)

BJÖRN
18

BENNY
17

AGNETHA
13

STIG
32

sets up Polar Music

plays keyboards with Elverkets Spelmanslag

forms Anni-Frid Four with fiancé Ragnar Fredricksson

1963

Björn and Anni-Frid enter same radio talent contest; neither wins, but Stig makes Björn's band his first signing at Polar Music, changing their name to Hootenanny Singers

1964

tours *folkparken* with Hootenanny Singers

joins Hep Stars

marries Ragnar Fredricksson

1965

appears with Hep Stars on Swedish TV; 'Cadillac' goes to No. 1; writes first song, 'No Response'

joins Bernt Enghardt's dance band

1970

release first single, 'She's My Kind of Girl'

Benny produces Anni-Frid's first album *Frida*; they move in together

releases first album *Frida;* single, 'Min egen Stad', goes to No. 1

1973

Record 'Ring, Ring'; goes to No. 1. Stig changes their name to ABBA

'Hej Gamle Man' from the album *Lycka,* first single featuring them all, goes to No. 1; perform first show as Festfolket

tour *folkparken*; Benny and Bjorn produce Agnetha's fourth album

get married

1972

assembles Björn & Benny, Agnetha & Anni-Frid

1971

1969

releases second album, *Agnetha Fältskog Volume II*

Björn moves in with Agnetha

Björn produces Agnetha's third album, *As I Am*

meet in Malmö

'Ljuva Sextital', first collaboration, reaches No. 2

receives Swedish Grammy

Hep Stars split up

plays *folkparken* with Lars Londahl

1968

releases first solo single, 'Raring'

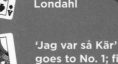

'Jag var så Kär' goes to No. 1; first album, *Agnetha Fältskog*

wins Sweden's *New Faces* TV show; releases first single, 'En ledig dag'

1966

breaks off engagement to Christina Grönvall

meet on the road; write first song together, 'It isn't Easy to Say'

writes 'Jag var så Kär'; signs with CBS-Cuprol label

1967

The Hootenanny Singers and the Hep Stars were the contrasting pillars of Sixties Swedish pop, and each contained a future member of ABBA. Björn co-founded folk-harmony foursome Hootenanny Singers and by 1963 was established as their frontman; and in 1964 Benny became the keyboard rock god of the wild bunch Hep Stars.

HOOTENANNY SINGERS

were polite, clean-cut, handsome young chaps. They wore suits and coordinated jumpers. They smoked pipes. They finished their university studies.

FOLK & POP

17 ALBUMS

34 SINGLES

First band signed to Stig Anderson's Polar Records

GREATEST HIT: 'Omkring tiggarn från Luossa' (charting from November 1972 to November 1973)

ACTIVE: **1961–75**

8 EP RECORDS

HOOTS V HEPS

POP, COUNTRY ROCK & ROCK 'N' ROLL

HEP STARS

were far more rock 'n' roll, teen idols with a Rolling Stones-style line-up. They despised uniforms, grew their hair long and were known as the Swedish Beatles, complete with ongoing musical differences and a shambolic Apple Corps-style management set-up they called Hep House.

ACTIVE: **1963–71**

8 NO. 1 SINGLES

12 ALBUMS

25 SINGLES

BENNY ANDERSSON

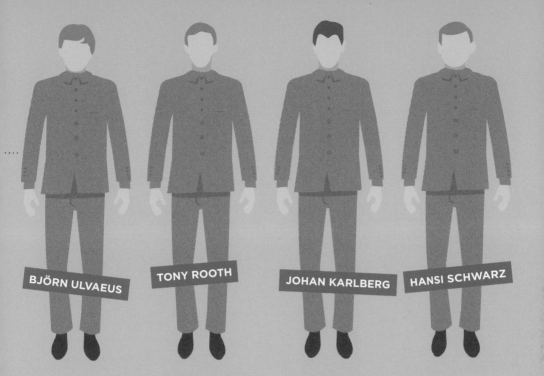

BJÖRN ULVAEUS TONY ROOTH JOHAN KARLBERG HANSI SCHWARZ

SVENNE HEDLUND CHRISTER PETTERSSON JANNE FRISK LENNART HEGLAND

SVENGALI STIG

Manager, guru, mentor and collaborator, the 'fifth ABBA' was an unstoppable combination of relentless ambition, energy, ego, talent, focus, self-confidence, marketing nous and ferocious work ethic: exactly how you would imagine a Viking impresario. Starting from nowhere and with nothing (the only child of a resourceful single mother), he bootstrapped himself to success by transmuting his love and talent for music – especially lyric writing – into an empire long before ABBA came along. His infallible ear for a hit, sharp eye for talent, unerring nose for opportunity and cheerfully outspoken disregard for convention led the rather stodgy Swedish musical establishment to sneeringly label him 'Mr Biz'. He took it as a compliment.

STIG ANDERSON

CLIENT: ABBA

ACTIVE: 1972–90

BACKGROUND: Musician, composer, entrepreneur

PASTORAL CARE

CONTROL OF PRIVATE LIFE

SENSITIVITY TO TALENT

FEE PERCENTAGE

EXPLOITATION

SVENGALI SCALE

	PASTORAL CARE	CONTROL OF PRIVATE LIFE	SENSITIVITY TO TALENT	FEE PERCENTAGE	EXPLOITATION

'COLONEL' TOM PARKER

CLIENT: Elvis Presley

ACTIVE: 1955–77

BACKGROUND:
Carnival huckster,
possibly on the run

BRIAN EPSTEIN

CLIENT: The Beatles

ACTIVE: 1961–7

BACKGROUND:
Businessman,
music shop owner

PETER GRANT

CLIENT: Led Zeppelin

ACTIVE: 1968–80

BACKGROUND:
Actor, wrestler,
tour manager

ASSEMBLING ABBA

You will need:

(A1)

1x **Brunette figure**

(A2)

1x **Blonde figure**

(B1)

1x **Bearded figure**

(B2)

1x **Non-bearded figure**

(K1)

(G1)

(K1)
1x **Keyboard**

(G1)
1x **Guitar**

(M1) (M2)
2x **Microphone**

(M1) **(M2)**

Not shown:

 (T) Talent

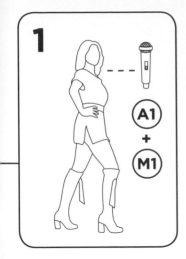

1 A1 + M1

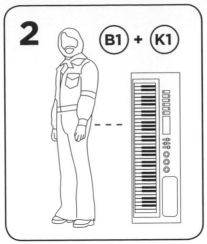

2 B1 + K1

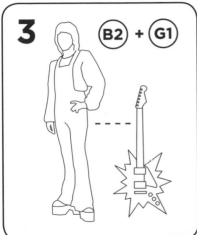

3 B2 + G1

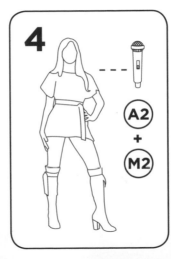

4 A2 + M2

STIG'S PUBLICITY PLOY

1. Decide on a band name – make it snappy, short, easy to say and international.

– – – – – – – – – –

2. Run a 'name-that-band' competition in a popular newspaper (*Göteborgs-Tidningen*, a daily evening paper in Gothenburg), which the name you have already chosen will win.

– – – – – – – – – –

3. Announce the winning name and launch the product.

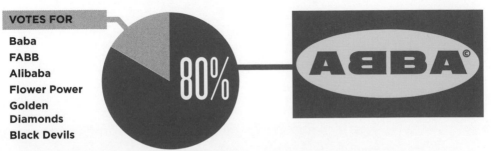

VOTES FOR

Baba
FABB
Alibaba
Flower Power
Golden Diamonds
Black Devils

80%

ABBA©

ABBA was already a brand name in Sweden, for a fish-canning company. When asked, they were happy to let ABBA use the name as long as they did not bring the herrings into disrepute. Brand synergy: fish lovers found ABBA the band and ABBA fans found a fish product. Win, win!

TYPECASTING

Clear, bold and deceptively simple, the ABBA logo stood like a Nordic rock in a frenetic sea of the glam, glitter and flamboyant flounces that flooded the 1970s. The clean, functional lines were a subtle indication that ABBA might sound all joyful froth, but they meant serious business. It was not just style; there was plenty of substance.

The ABBA logo is a faithful representation of the group's dynamic. They were equals: friends, collaborators and finally married couples. Each letter has the same weight and size; there is no preferential hierarchy. The reversal of the first 'B' presents a pared-down image of two strong couples facing each other in line against the world; and in the middle sits the couple that lasted, Benny and Björn, the songwriting engine at the heart of the band.

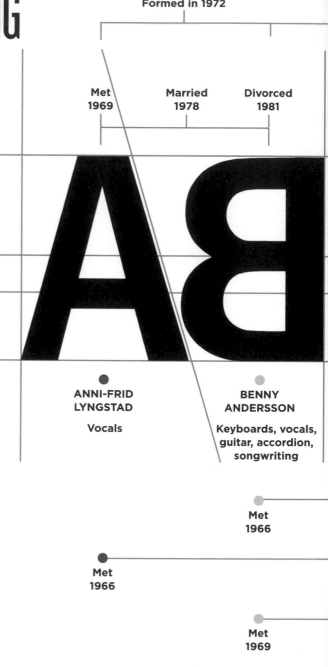

Formed in 1972

Met 1969   Married 1978   Divorced 1981

ANNI-FRID LYNGSTAD

Vocals

BENNY ANDERSSON

Keyboards, vocals, guitar, accordion, songwriting

Met 1966

Met 1966

Met 1969

Met 1968

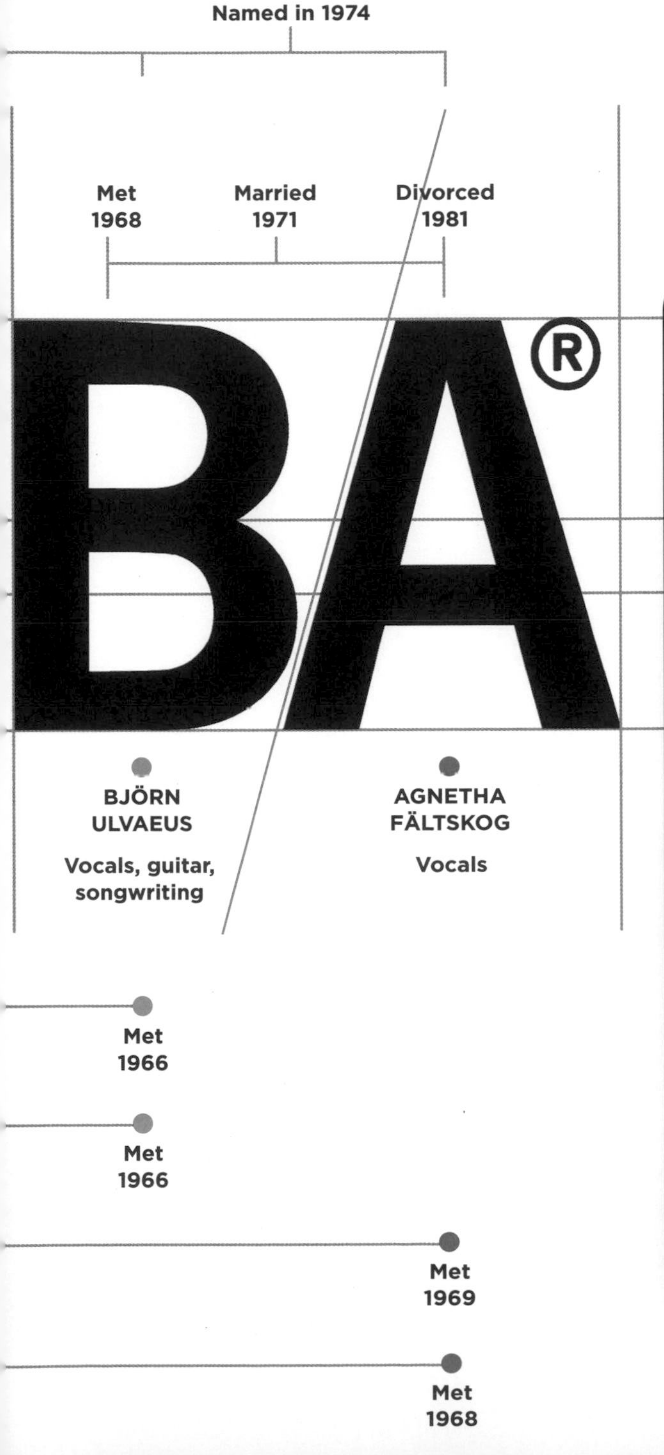

Named in 1974

Met
1968

Married
1971

Divorced
1981

BA®

ABBA LOGO

A triumph of impactful branding, the ABBA logo – with its disruptive reversed 'B' – was designed by Rune Söderqvist (1935–2014) using News Gothic Bold. This is a sans serif font originally designed by American typeface design supremo Morris Fuller Benton (1872–1948) and released by American Type Founders in 1908. News Gothic is a classic typeface with great staying power and versatility. Versions of it were much used in magazines and newspapers throughout the 20th century.

The logo first appeared in May 1976, and was used throughout the band's career across all platforms and sizes, also appearing in lights in their stage set.

**BJÖRN
ULVAEUS**

Vocals, guitar,
songwriting

**AGNETHA
FÄLTSKOG**

Vocals

Met
1966

Met
1966

Met
1969

Met
1968

DRESS LIKE ABBA

Breathe in. Learn to love Lycra, polyester and satin, and twirling in a cloud of glitter. Wear everything as eye-wateringly tight and shiny as possible, add some swirly capes for extra stage impact and practise dancing in platforms without falling over.

ABBA were not the first (nor the last) on the glam rock scene; others may have done it more stylishly, but they were the band that made outrageous, cheesy outfits synonymous with their brand and stage act. Their costume designer, Owe Sandström (b. 1944) made clothes that reflected song themes or tipped a velvet fedora to the culture of the countries they toured (as well as emphasizing Anni-Frid's and Agnetha's figures – well, it was 1974...). Sandström was, and is, immensely proud of his memorable creations, although Björn had his doubts (see below). Underneath all that spangly spandex was a sensible business strategy. The band could claim tax relief on their stage clothes as they were demonstrably so bizarre and outlandish that no-one sane would wear them in the street. Smart move.

"IN MY HONEST OPINION WE LOOKED LIKE NUTS IN THOSE YEARS. NOBODY CAN HAVE BEEN AS BADLY DRESSED ON STAGE AS WE WERE."

—Björn Ulvaeus, taken from *ABBA: The Official Photo Book*, 2014

Micro mini dress

Catsuit

Blouson jacket

Jumpsuit

Scarf

Cape

Knee-high boots

Bell bottoms

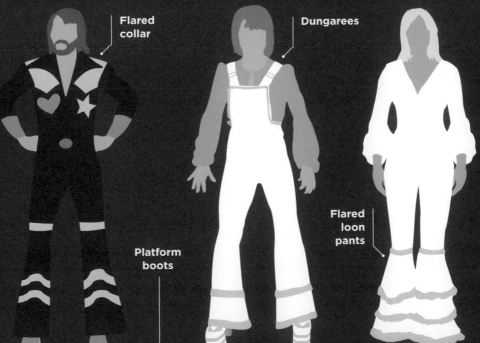

Flared collar

Dungarees

Platform boots

Flared loon pants

WATERLOO

1st example of a choreographed act

1st Eurovision win for Sweden

1st winning entry not sung in a native language

1st song released from ABBA's second album, *Waterloo*

In 1974, hosted by the UK in Brighton, the Eurovision Song Contest provided a springboard to international fame for ABBA. They went at it full tilt, storming the stage in their flamboyant outfits, full of joyful energy. Their conductor, Sven-Olof Walldoff, came on dressed as Napoleon, and ABBA won with 'Waterloo', an upbeat celebration of love as a battlefield. 'Waterloo' went to the top of the charts all over Europe and beyond. At the 50th Anniversary Eurovision Jubilee, it was voted the best song in the competition's history.

The joyful kitschfest that is Eurovision was originally set up as a peacemongering project in 1955. It was a Swiss initiative to bring a still war-scarred Europe together by fostering cooperation and exploiting music's capacity to soothe and unify. The first contest was held in 1956 in Lugano, Switzerland (they won; there's a thing!), with seven entries. As of 2019, 50 countries were eligible to take part.

EUROVISION SONG CONTEST 1974

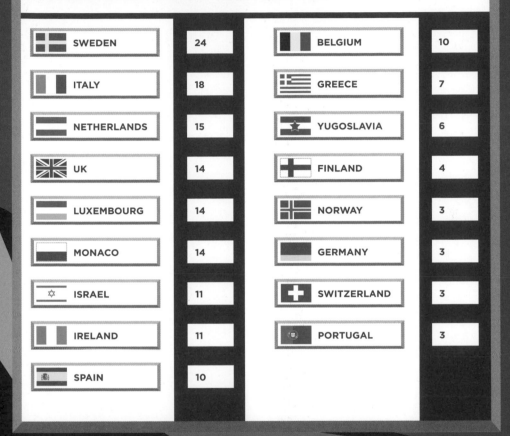

🇸🇪 SWEDEN	24	
ITALY	18	
NETHERLANDS	15	
UK	14	
LUXEMBOURG	14	
MONACO	14	
ISRAEL	11	
IRELAND	11	
SPAIN	10	
BELGIUM	10	
GREECE	7	
YUGOSLAVIA	6	
FINLAND	4	
NORWAY	3	
GERMANY	3	
SWITZERLAND	3	
PORTUGAL	3	

WATERLOO FACTS

- Written in 1973 specifically for the contest
- Lyrics by Stig Anderson, the band's manager
- Original title was 'Honey Pie'
- First song released by ABBA under their new name
- Influenced by 'See My Baby Jive' (1973) by Wizzard
- Instantly topped the UK charts and stayed there for two weeks
- Topped the charts in Belgium, Denmark, Finland, West Germany, Ireland, Norway, South Africa and Switzerland

6 MILLION
copies of 'Waterloo' sold

THANK YOU FOR THE MUSIC

ABBA did not break up in a hail of writs and acrimony; no-one stormed out in a blaze of Viking rage and broke the band up – they just lost the will to go on. After a decade of living and working together, they had run out of steam. By 1982, both couples had split up, giving the fairy tale an unhappy ending. Benny and Björn were both expectant fathers with their new partners. All of them wanted to move on to new adventures. There was no formal announcement; they simply stopped and efficiently disassembled themselves, leaving fans with a tiny hope that they might, one day, put themselves back together again.

LAST STUDIO ALBUM:
The Visitors
November 1981

LAST PERFORMANCE IN SWEDEN:
Nöjesmaskinen,
('The Entertainment Machine')
Swedish TV
19 November 1982

LAST SINGLE RELEASED:
'Under Attack'
December 1982

LAST PERFORMANCE:
(via satellite link)
The Late Late Breakfast Show
UK TV
11 December 1982

ABBA

02
WORLD

"IN SWEDEN,
STARDOM IS
LOOKED UPON
AS PHONEY.

YOU WALK TO THE THEATRE EVERY DAY LIKE EVERYBODY ELSE."

—Lena Olin, Swedish actress and wife of ABBA's video director Lasse Hallström, *Los Angeles Times*, 1993

LAGOM

Adjective

ENGLISH TRANSLATION:
Just right

EXTRAVAGANCE

PLAY

BLING

SUCCESS

ARROGANCE

WEALTH

HEDONISM

MORE IS MORE

EXCESS

FIRE

LIGHT

PLEASURE

SEX

JUST

Lagom means balance, moderation, appropriateness. It is a shaping concept in the Swedish psyche, in which moderation is pursued rather than success; both perfectionism and fecklessness are shunned. The sweet spot in the middle is the goal: an elegant sufficiency. ABBA suffered rather in their home country, as they were seen by some as aiming for too much (be it international success, money or the perfect sound) and criticized for it. As the Swedes say, 'Lagom är bäst', meaning the right amount is best, or 'Enough is as good as a feast'.

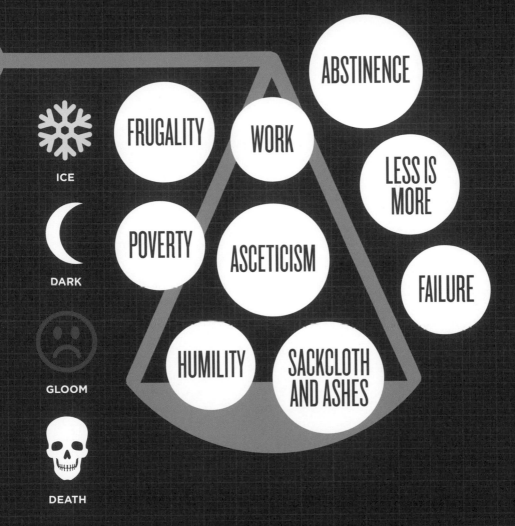

ICE

DARK

GLOOM

DEATH

ABSTINENCE

FRUGALITY

WORK

LESS IS MORE

POVERTY

ASCETICISM

FAILURE

HUMILITY

SACKCLOTH AND ASHES

RIGHT

PROGG

Progg was the polar opposite of ABBA. An entirely Swedish phenomenon, it is short for *progressiv musik*, a left-wing movement using music as a political medium that peaked about the same time as ABBA were going global. Proggs despised ABBA for their slick production values, pop aesthetic and lack of political engagement or serious message. Its proponents were mainly ex-hippies and Sixties radicals, much influenced by pre-electric Dylan and American protest music.

Hoola Bandoola Band

SANG IN
SWEDISH

PUNK
MUSICIANS

5 STUDIO RECORDINGS

STOCKHOLM

MALMÖ

The combination of punk ideology (musical talent was distrusted and subordinate to the message) and political polemic was very popular in Sweden, and the leading lights were the Hoola Bandoola Band. Interestingly, Stig Anderson, with his unerring nose for a moneymaking trend, tried to sign them up to Polar Records, but the cultural dissonance proved too much.

4 MEMBERS

SANG IN
ENGLISH

7 MEMBERS

COMMERCIAL
FRIVOLOUS
PROFESSIONAL
AMBITIOUS
APOLITICAL
CYNICAL
EXPLOITATIVE
ENTERTAINING
SUPERFICIAL
PRAGMATIC

PROFESSIONAL
MUSICIANS

8 STUDIO ALBUMS

NOT FOR PROFIT
RADICAL
AMATEUR
REVOLUTIONARY
POLEMICAL
SINCERE
EDUCATIONAL
SERIOUS
PROFOUND
PURIST

ABBA

LOVE ISLANDS

Despite a low population density, many Swedes – especially in the more crowded south – appear to long for solitude and a break from their compatriots. Swedish-born Greta Garbo was not alone in wanting to be alone. The most popular choice of bolthole is an island, of which Sweden has a substantial supply. Many Swedes own a summer cabin on an island, or in some cases a whole island. The members of ABBA were no exception, and islands featured strongly in their lives and careers.

The Stockholm archipelago is made up of approximately

24,000

islands.

STOCKHOLM COUNTY

VIGGSÖ

STOCKHOLM

There are over

50,000

holiday homes in the archipelago.

VIGGSÖ

1970:
Stig Anderson buys a holiday cottage.

1971:
Björn and Agnetha buy a house and attached cottage.

1974:
Benny and Anni-Frid buy a holiday cottage.

Benny and Björn used Björn's cottage as a tranquil base for songwriting; they composed 'Ring, Ring' here, and later worked on 'Dancing Queen', 'Fernando' and others. A replica of the cottage can be seen in the ABBA museum in Stockholm.

POPULATION DENSITY

Number of people per square kilometre:

❶ 25   **❷** 36

❸ 274   **❹** 488

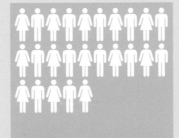

❶ SWEDEN

❷ USA

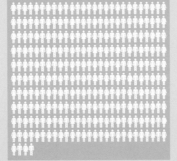

❸ UK

❹ NETHERLANDS

PARK LIFE

The *folkpark* or *folkets park* – meaning 'people's park' – is central to Swedish life. Every town has one, some big cities have more. Most were set up in the early 20th century, to provide green space and fresh air for all. They were a place for entertainment, public meeting and recreation, often with a stage or bandstand.

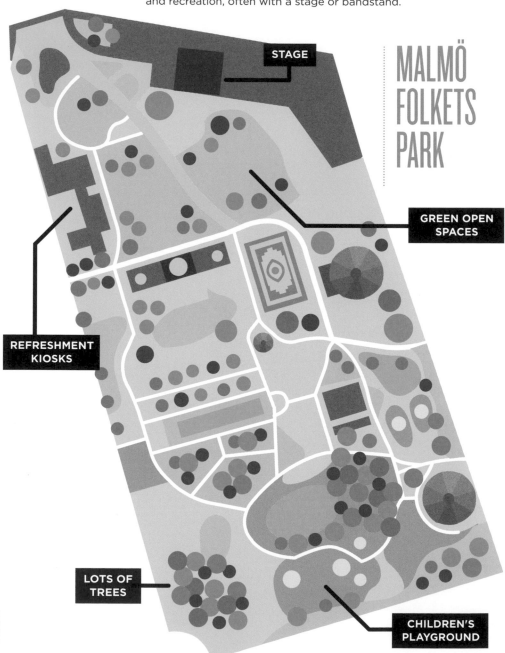

STAGE

MALMÖ FOLKETS PARK

GREEN OPEN SPACES

REFRESHMENT KIOSKS

LOTS OF TREES

CHILDREN'S PLAYGROUND

Almost every Swedish pop act paid their dues working the *folkpark* circuit. ABBA certainly did, as individual artists and as a group, even after they had gone global. The parks were a kind of wholesome alfresco version of the seedy subterranean Hamburg cellars that bred The Beatles. No one much liked playing them – the facilities were often poor, the acoustics unsatisfactory and the pay risible – but everyone did it because the *folkpark* circuit offered a national showcase and an unparalleled networking opportunity.

Touring was always in summer and early autumn (June to September) because of light levels and temperatures. The shows went on all day to make the best of the long days of a short summer.

North of the Arctic Circle, the sun does not set between the end of May and mid-July and does not rise between the end of November and mid-January.

JAN FEB MAR APR MAY JUN JUL AUG SEP OCT NOV DEC

BJÖRN & BENNY, AGNETHA & ANNI-FRID **1973**

FOLKPARK TOUR 15 JUNE TO 9 SEPTEMBER

66 CONCERTS
12 SONGS

23 JUNE 1973

ABBA visited Överkalix and Tärendö, which would have had perpetual daylight at this time of year.

ABBA FOLKPARK TOUR

21 JUNE TO 9 JULY 1975

14 CONCERTS 16 SONGS

SCHLAGER LOUTS

Schlager, the German word for 'hit' or 'beat', is the name for the popular music style that emerged between the two world wars in Germany and rapidly spread to northern and central Europe, later slipping southwards. The spectacularly uncool lovechild of folk music, operetta, cabaret and music hall, it features simple, earwormy tunes with an irresistible clap-along beat beneath sentimental, sometimes imbecilic lyrics on banal, uncontroversial themes. 'Dum Dum Diddle', anyone? ABBA grew up listening to Swedish schlager, the heartbeat of the *folkpark* circuit, ingested the genre, subtly infused it with disco, rock and dark matter and transmuted it into gold.

HOW TO BUILD A SWEDISH SCHLAGER SONG

Swedish schlager songs are engineered to Eurovision parameters. Listen to ABBA's 'Money, Money, Money' to see how they did it.

HARDWARE

 Drums   **Guitars**   **Keyboard**    **Accordion**   **Vocals**

SOFTWARE

 Clap-along beat   **Simple catchy tune**   **Killer-hook chorus**   **Key change**    **Easy lyrics**

TOPICS

Select one uncontroversial subject:

 Love   **Holidays**   **Pets**   **Nonsense**

PROCESS

= handclapping beat

for a three-minute duration

Select one of...

Use an Allen key to insert

Insert

MELODIFESTIVALEN

Melodifestivalen (sometimes called Mellofest), the annual competition to choose the Swedish Eurovision entry, is nicknamed the Schlagerfestival. In ABBA's time, it was a simple, one-off competition judged by a panel of experts and music critics.

Apply

Add lots of orchestration and clap along to your schlager song.

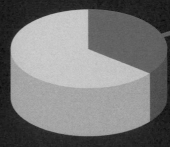

36%

of the Swedish population watched Mellofest 2019.

GLAM ROCKS!

By the time ABBA burst onto the international stage in a cloud of glitter, glam rock had been a dominant force on the UK pop scene for some years. Kicked off in 1971 by Marc Bolan of T. Rex, who appeared bespangled and electrifying on the UK television show *Top of the Pops* performing 'Get it On', the style flourished briefly and brightly until 1975. Instantly misunderstood by many irate parents as effeminacy gone mad, glam rock was a performative style based on circus acts, drag artists, stage performance and the contemporary interest in shape-shifting, role-playing and androgyny. And there was a practical motivation – glitter and satin look great under lights on a big stage. There is a reason why trapeze artists wear spangly tights.

BRYAN FERRY AND ROXY MUSIC
1970–6

ZIGGY STARDUST
AND THE SPIDERS
FROM MARS
1972–3

KISS
1973–PRESENT

ABBA

ABBA were more glam pop really: after all, they had two girls in the band, and truly transgressive glam rock was an all-boy thing. Rock bands in the UK and US expressed their glam in various ways. Their fans followed suit.

 ART-SCHOOL GLAM
Cool, glamorous, louche, sophisticated and ironic, with a hint of cabaret.

 PERFORMANCE GLAM
Transgressive, theatrical, liminal, narrative with a nod to Brecht.

 METAL GLAM
Theatrical, playful, bombastic, gothic, shocking, with a hint of Hollywood horror.

ROCK GLAM
Fun, friendly, raucous, blokeish pantomime, with a hint of transgressive stag-do.

BUBBLEGUM GLAM
Naughty, poppy, parodic, light-hearted, comedic, with a hint of British music hall.

SLADE
1970–4

THE SWEET
1971–8

HOUSEHOLD ICONS

For a small country, with a population about the same as London, Sweden has had a big impact on the world, particularly in the spheres of design, engineering and electronics. While ABBA were imposing their logo on the world of international pop, other industries were busy making, expanding or reinforcing their own marks.

🔳 **Electrolux**

VOLVO

FOUNDED
1876, Stockholm

FOUNDER
Lars Magnus Ericsson

BUSINESS
Telecommunications and software company

FOUNDED
1919, Stockholm

FOUNDER
Axel Wenner-Gren

BUSINESS
Domestic appliance manufacturer; consistently the second largest in the world

FOUNDED
1927, Gothenburg

FOUNDERS
Assar Gabrielsson, Gustaf Larson

BUSINESS
Car manufacturing company with a mission to make safety the first priority; its name is Latin for 'I roll'

Tetra Pak

FOUNDED
1937, Linköping

FOUNDERS
Marcus Wallenberg Jr., Axel Wenner-Gren, Sven Gustaf Wingqvist

BUSINESS
Aerospace and defence company Svenska Aeroplan AB, parent company to SAAB Automobile, whose first car rolled off the line in 1949

FOUNDED
1943, Elmtaryd Farm, Agunnaryd

FOUNDER
Ingvar Kamprad

BUSINESS
The world's most ubiquitous furniture and lifestyle retailer

FOUNDED
1951, Lund

FOUNDER
Ruben Rausing

BUSINESS
Food-packaging empire, based on Erik Wallenberg's invention of a tetrahedron design in plastic-coated cardboard

ABBA

03
WORK

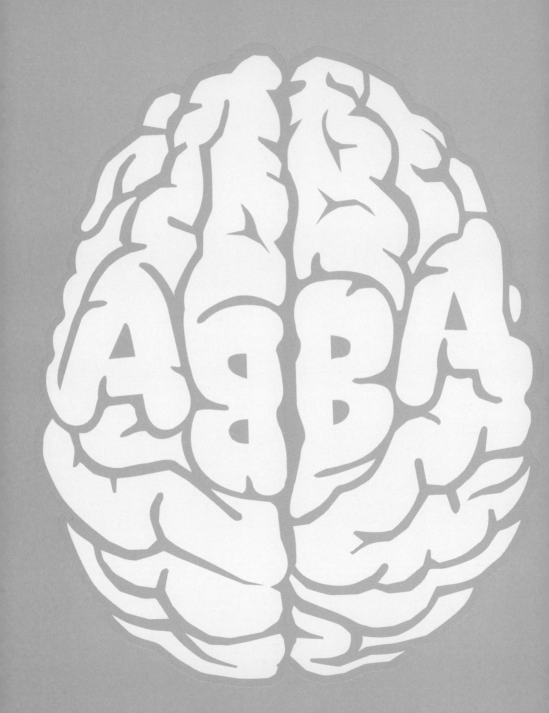

"ABBA SONGS, AS ANYONE WHO KNOWS KNOWS, ARE CONSTRUCTED, TECHNICALLY AND HARMONICALLY, SO AS TO PHYSICALLY IMPRINT THE HUMAN BRAIN AS IF BITING IT WITH ACID, TO ENSURE WE WILL NEVER, EVER, EVER BE ABLE TO FORGET THEM."

—Miles Garth, taken from Ali Smith's novel *There But for The*, 2011

WRITING A SONG WITH BENNY AND BJÖRN*

*AND OCCASIONALLY STIG

Go there, taking your instruments.

YOU ARE BENNY.

Play around with some chords until you get a progression and/or rhythm you like. Play it to Björn. Does he like it?

YES

YES

NO

YES

START

Do you own an island with a summer house on it?

Do you have a beard, keyboard skills and innate musicality?

Refine and reduce. Does he like it now?

NO

NO

NO

YES

Find a hotel room, disused warehouse or office building open after hours.

Are you clean-shaven? Do you also own a guitar and amp, and sing well?

Noodle on your guitar looking for a melody or hook. Play it to Benny. Does he like it?

YES

YOU ARE BJÖRN.

Benny and Björn both acknowledged Lennon and McCartney as inspiration and encouragement for their collaborative songwriting. "If they can do it," mused Björn, "then so can we." In the main, Benny was about the music, melody, sound and mood, and Björn was about the words and the story, but it is the collaboration that creates the end result. They wrote their first song together in 1966 when they were a Hep Star and a Hootenanny Singer. Here's how to do it. You will need a partner.

Using the 'Scrambled egg'/'Yesterday' method pioneered by McCartney, insert nonsense lyrics as placeholders.

Is it after 1966 but before 1976?

YES

YES

NO

Repeat until you get a whole song with verse, chorus and optional middle eight. Do you both agree on the end product?

Discard and start again.

NO

Take the song to Stig Anderson, who will provide a Europop lyric in English and a killer international title.

NO

BJÖRN

BENNY

Start again.

Write your own lyrics. Show them to Benny. If he doesn't like them, rewrite them.

Concentrate on orchestration and sound.

Record the song.

WHO SANG WHAT?

Anni-Frid and Agnetha faced each other as they sang so that they could check lip synchronization and signal to each other.

Anni-Frid sang lead on

25

tracks.

SHOWSTOPPERS: 'Money, Money, Money', 'Knowing Me, Knowing You', 'Super Trouper'

51
TRACKS

were sung together, either in harmony or in unison, or taking alternate verse and chorus.

In 1972, after recording 'People Need Love', Benny realized that what was unique about the ABBA sound was the combination of the two female voices. He and Björn now stepped back from the mics, apart from some chorus work and harmonizing. This gave Agnetha and Anni-Frid the freedom to sing together, in harmony, in unison, separately and alternately, and double-tracked with themselves. And they didn't just sing what they were told: they made significant contributions to harmonies, phrasing, delivery and how to shape a song. In recordings until 1975, the vocal tracks were added last. After this, as the songs became more intricate, the vocal track went into the mix earlier and the backing track was refined, expanded or contracted to complement it.

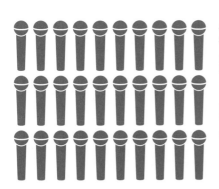

Agnetha sang lead on

30

tracks.

SHOWSTOPPERS: 'SOS', 'Gimme! Gimme! Gimme!', 'The Winner Takes it All'

Agnetha is a soprano with a typical range of two octaves from middle C to high C, while Anni-Frid is a mezzo-soprano with a typical range of two octaves from the A below middle C (A3) to the A above it (A5). The two voices are nearly but not quite matched, so when they sing in unison they create a special, intimate sound.

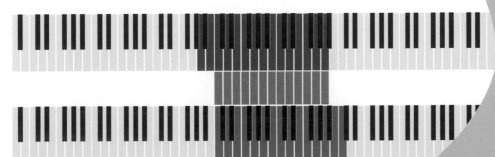

IN THE STUDIO

At Metronome Studios, and later Polar Studios, producer Michael B. Tretow used a 24-track machine (later 32-track) and usually did the backing tracks first. This established the mood of the song before the vocals were added.

Benny and Björn knew their way around a studio (they had already produced records for themselves and for Agnetha and Anni-Frid as solo artists, among others), but Benny wanted to find a way to create the sound that was in his head. His idol was Brian Wilson of the Beach Boys, and he was seeking Beach Boy levels of perfectionism and a dense, detailed sound. In January 1973, he and Björn began working with sound engineer Michael B. Tretow, who introduced them to Phil Spector's concept of the Wall of Sound. Together they forged the unique ABBA sound, a blend of intricate, ethereal Wilsonian harmonies, thundering multi-layered instrumentation, unlikely instruments and the blending voices of Agnetha and Anni-Frid, all underpinned by a schlager-funk beat.

◀ **Michael B. Tretow, ABBA's producer**

DAY ONE
TRACKS 1–6

1 Record in drum booth, not in main room.

2 **3** **4** Record in separate room, if available, with amp as loud as possible to get the 'box of noise' effect.

5 Record using three mics: top, middle and bottom.

6 Record using ambient mic only.

END OF DAY

Overdub everything.

Slow down speed by 0.5%.

DAY TWO
TRACKS 7–15

7 **8** **9** **10** **11** **12** **13** **14** Try different tempos, moods and instrumentation until satisfied.

15 Record guide vocals by Agnetha, Anni-Frid or Björn, using nonsense lyrics.

DAY FOUR
TRACKS 23–24

23 **24**
Record lead vocals with final lyrics using single stereo mic.

19 **20** **21** **22**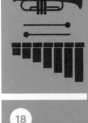
Record brass, marimba, xylophone, glockenspiel, etc., as needed, and overdub.

18
Record percussion and overdub.

17
If possible, record background unison singing in isolation room using ceiling stereo mic for big sound.

Double-track with speed variations.

16
Record backing harmonies using stereo mics.

Double-track with speed variations.

DAY THREE
TRACKS 16–22

DAY FIVE: THE MIX

Mix down in this order:

DRUMS

PERCUSSION

PIANO

GUITAR

BASS

SYNTH

BACKING VOCALS

FINAL SONG ◯
VOCALS

THE ABBA SOUND

Tretow double-tracked vocal and instrumental tracks with a slight time lag of 0.5%, which altered the pitch and instantly transformed two voices into a choir or one guitar into an orchestra. This gave more depth to the final recording and became a signature ABBA technique.

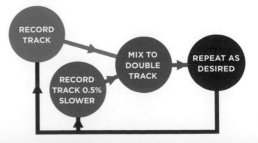

RECORD TRACK

MIX TO DOUBLE TRACK

REPEAT AS DESIRED

RECORD TRACK 0.5% SLOWER

WORK

59

ANATOMY OF AN ALBUM: ARRIVAL

ABBA's fourth studio album, just over a year in the making, landed in October 1976. Aptly titled *Arrival*, it is considered retrospectively to be their masterpiece, yet at the time it was damned with faint praise by a number of music critics, especially at home in Sweden. Everybody else loved it. Diverse, eclectic, accomplished and confident, the album propelled the band to worldwide superstardom. It featured an instrumental, a rare country-style solo by Björn and three whopper hits; and the iconic cover (designed by Rune Söderqvist), with its eerie space-bubble helicopter shot, saw the first outing for the new ABBA logo with the mirrored 'B'.

WHOPPER HITS

The first track laid down, this magnificent glitterball of Europop disco was released as a single on 15 August 1976.

A heart-piercing break-up song, it was released as a single in February 1977 and was the UK's biggest selling single that year.

Released as a single on 1 November 1976, it was No. 1 in Australia and most of Europe, and No. 3 in the UK.

SIDE A

1) When I Kissed the Teacher
2) Dancing Queen
3) My Love, My Life
4) Dum Dum Diddle
5) Knowing Me, Knowing You

The Australian and New Zealand versions had an extra track, 'Fernando'.

ABBA
• ARRIVAL

RUNTIME:

37:31

MINS   SECS

SIDE B

6) Money, Money, Money
7) That's Me
8) Why Did it Have to be Me?
9) Tiger
10) Arrival (Ode to Dalecarlia)

The final track on *Arrival* is one of only two ABBA instrumental tracks (although it does have a vocal chorus).

WHO WROTE WHAT?

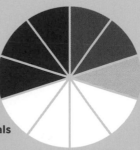

BENNY & BJÖRN
5
5
BENNY, BJÖRN & STIG

The famous cover shot was photographed at Barkarby Airport near Stockholm, with the band in the cockpit of a Bell 47 helicopter.

WHO SANG WHAT?

- ● Anni-Frid lead vocals
- ● Agnetha lead vocals
- ● Björn lead vocals
- ○ Anni-Frid and Agnetha co-vocals

SALES FIGURES

 NO. 1

1,500,000

No. 1 for 12 weeks.

1,000,000

500,000

UK · W. GERMANY · AUSTRALIA · POLAND · SWEDEN · JAPAN · NETHERLANDS · USA · DENMARK · CANADA

RING, RING *
1973

Only released in Australia, Mexico, South Africa, Sweden and West Germany

●●●●●● — Single
●●●●●● — Track

SINGLES:
'Ring, Ring', 'People Need Love', 'Nina, Pretty Ballerina', 'Love isn't Easy', 'He is Your Brother'

WATERLOO
1974

Features two versions of 'Waterloo', one in Swedish, one in English

●●●●●●
●●●●●●

SINGLES:
'Waterloo', 'Honey, Honey'

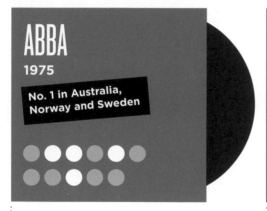

ABBA
1975

No. 1 in Australia, Norway and Sweden

●●●●●
●●●●●

SINGLES:
'Mamma Mia', 'SOS', 'Bang-a-Boomerang', 'I Do, I Do, I Do', 'Rock Me', 'I've Been Waiting for You', 'So Long'

ARRIVAL
1976

No. 1 in Australia, Netherlands, New Zealand, Norway, Sweden and UK

●●●●●
●●●●●

SINGLES:
'Dancing Queen', 'Knowing Me, Knowing You', 'Money, Money, Money', 'That's Me' (in Japan only)

*Recorded as Björn & Benny, Agnetha & Anni-Frid

THE ALBUMS

ABBA were essentially a studio band, and their eight studio albums chart a trajectory from cheerful schlager/folk fusion via Europop and international disco to something darker. None are concept albums, but each has a prevailing mood, forming the soundtrack to a great love affair going from innocent adoration via intense excitement to world-weary maturity. They also released two indifferent live albums and seven compilations. The last of these, the stupendous yet post-break-up collection of their best tracks, *ABBA Gold*, was released in 1992 and has been selling like hot *kanelbullar* (cinnamon buns) ever since.

ABBA: THE ALBUM
1977 (Sweden) 1978 (UK)

No. 1 in eight countries, including UK

SINGLES:
'Take a Chance on Me', 'The Name of the Game', 'Thank You for the Music'

VOULEZ-VOUS
1979

No. 1 in Finland, Japan, Netherlands, Norway, Sweden, UK and West Germany

SINGLES:
'Voulez-Vous', 'I Have a Dream', 'Does Your Mother Know', 'Chiquitita'

SUPER TROUPER
1980

No. 1 in Netherlands, Norway, Sweden, UK and West Germany

SINGLES:
'Super Trouper', 'The Winner Takes It All', 'On and On and On', 'Andante, Andante', 'Happy New Year', 'Our Last Summer', 'Lay all Your Love on Me'

THE VISITORS
1981

No. 1 in Finland, Japan, Netherlands, Norway, Sweden, UK and West Germany

SINGLES:
'The Visitors', 'Head over Heels', 'When All is Said and Done', 'One of Us', 'Slipping through My Fingers'

ABBA GOLD...

Second best-selling album of all time

is the group's highest-selling album, and shot the band to prominence a decade after their break-up. All other compilations were deleted, leaving only the eight studio albums and the live album in the catalogue. It went gold itself on its 10th anniversary release in 2002.

1991

TRACKS:
19

WORLDWIDE SALES:
30 million

UK SALES:
5.5 million

First popular music CD to be pressed at Phillips Polydor plant in Germany in 1983, although not the first to be produced (that was Claudio Arrau playing Chopin waltzes) or released (that was Billy Joel's *52nd Street* in October 1982).

ANATOMY OF A SINGLE: DANCING QUEEN

RUNTIME:

03:52

MINS   SECS

Often called the perfect pop song, 'Dancing Queen' was recorded in 1975 but not released until August 1976 (shelved in favour of Stig Anderson's preferred 'Fernando'), when it smashed its way to number one in 16 countries. Almost half a century later, it's still the world's favourite floor-filler, the track you can't sit down to. With a lilting, relaxed rhythm, it appeals to almost everybody, transcending cool/cheesy categorization. It was Senator John McCain's favourite song, Dave Grohl of the Foo Fighters adores it, Elvis Costello stole its descending piano chords for 'Oliver's Army', and Anni-Frid burst into tears when she first heard the backing track. It is ABBA's glittering, shimmering, impregnable, indestructible, quintessential masterpiece.

TIME LINE

1975

4 AUGUST
Recording starts

SEPTEMBER
Agnetha and Anni-Frid record vocals

DECEMBER
First half of second verse edited out

1976

16 AUGUST
Single released

18 JUNE
Performed for marriage of King Carl XVI Gustaf to Silvia Sommerlath

JANUARY
Performed in Germany

1977

APRIL
Becomes ABBA's only No. 1 single in the US

1993 DECEMBER
Anni-Frid and The Real Group perform the song for Queen Silvia's 50th birthday

2015

Song inducted into Grammy Hall of Fame

WRITERS:
Benny, Björn and Stig

INFLUENCES:
'Rock Your Baby' by George McCrae (1974)

Dr John's Gumbo **by Dr John (1972)**

Backwards 'B' logo on a single for the first time

KEY:

A

BPM:

101

NO. 1 IN **16** COUNTRIES

Australia
Belgium
Brazil
Canada
Ireland
Japan
Mexico
Netherlands
New Zealand
Norway
South Africa
Sweden
UK
USA
West Germany
Zimbabwe

3 MILLION COPIES SOLD

VIDEO: **Directed by Lasse Hallström**

Recorded at Alexandra's Disco, Stockholm

408 MILLION YOUTUBE VIEWS

B-SIDE:

'That's Me'

THE SINGLES

Picking up where The Beatles left off, ABBA excelled in precision-engineering the perfect pop single: around three minutes long with a killer hook, a couple of verses and a singalong chorus. They were an astounding global success, but were far more than a cynical production line for static, mindless bounciness. Without swapping genres, they evolved and took their listeners with them. As they matured, each song became like a small slice of a saga, a glimpse of a bigger story behind it. The band that could sing 'Bang-a-Boomerang' without irony in 1975 were able to perfectly articulate grown-up, complicated heartbreak five years later in 'The Winner Takes it All', the saddest and most heartfelt break-up song in pop music.

2
TAKE A
CHANCE ON ME
★ ★ ★

3
FERNANDO
★ ★ ★ ★
★ ★ ★

4
MAMMA MIA
★ ★ ★ ★

5
SUPER
TROUPER
★ ★ ★ ★

ABBA HAD 19 CONSECUTIVE TOP 10 HITS IN THE UK ALONE

6
MONEY, MONEY,
MONEY
★ ★ ★ ★

7
KNOWING ME,
KNOWING YOU
★ ★ ★

10
I HAVE
A DREAM
★ ★

8
CHIQUITITA
★ ★ ★

9
ONE OF US
★ ★ ★

11
THE NAME
OF THE GAME
★

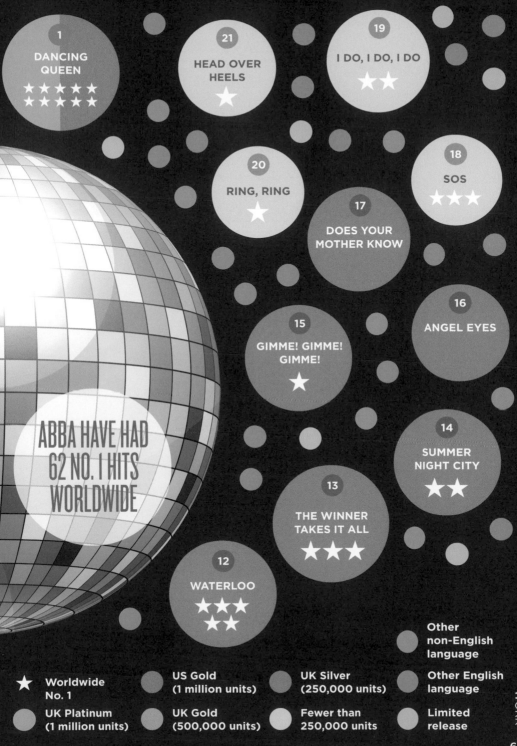

1 DANCING QUEEN
★★★★★
★★★★★

21 HEAD OVER HEELS
★

19 I DO, I DO, I DO
★★

20 RING, RING
★

18 SOS
★★★

17 DOES YOUR MOTHER KNOW

16 ANGEL EYES

15 GIMME! GIMME! GIMME!
★

ABBA HAVE HAD 62 NO. 1 HITS WORLDWIDE

14 SUMMER NIGHT CITY
★★

13 THE WINNER TAKES IT ALL
★★★

12 WATERLOO
★★★
★★

★ Worldwide No. 1

UK Platinum (1 million units)

US Gold (1 million units)

UK Gold (500,000 units)

UK Silver (250,000 units)

Fewer than 250,000 units

Other non-English language

Other English language

Limited release

ALL I DO IS EAT AND SLEEP AND SING

Maybe they were wearied by the 'before-they-were-ABBA' slogs round the Swedish *folkpark* circuit, maybe they missed home, maybe they found the crowds oppressive, but ABBA did not enjoy touring. It did not seem to energize them, and their live albums reflect this. Agnetha didn't like leaving her babies, Benny found life on the road monotonous, Björn thought it killed creativity; maybe only Anni-Frid, with her more cabaret-style background and love of performance, got very much out of it. Nevertheless, they toured at home and all over Europe, the USA, Australia and Japan. They did it as a thank you to their fans, because they were professional and industrious, and because Stig Anderson insisted, but it bored them: their hearts were in the studio.

ABBA were booked for two concerts at London's Royal Albert Hall on 14 February 1977; 3.5 million fans applied for tickets. The Albert Hall's current seating capacity is 5,272, slightly less than the 1970s, but even so, to satisfy demand ABBA would have had to play **664** concerts.

NO. OF TOURS:

8

Although ABBA paid their dues, their number of tour dates pales into insignificance compared to the true road warriors...

174
(1973–82)

1,400
(1961–66)

2,000
(1962–present)

3,000
('Never Ending Tour', 1988–present)

1973* — 66 concerts

FOLKPARK TOUR
(15 June–
9 September)

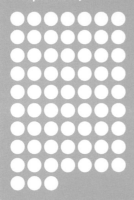

1974 — 14 concerts

TOUR OF NORTHERN EUROPE
(22 October–
30 November)

1975 — 7 concerts

SCANDINAVIAN TOUR
(10–22 January)

1977 — 15 concerts

EUROPEAN TOUR
(28 January–
14 February)

1975 — 14 concerts

FOLKPARK TOUR
(21 June–9 July)

🏠 Home preview
✕ Cancelled

1977 — 8 concerts

AUSTRALIAN TOUR
(3–12 March)

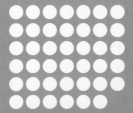

1980 — 11 concerts

JAPANESE TOUR
(12–27 March)

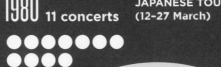

*Touring
as Björn
& Benny,
Agnetha
& Anni-Frid

1979 — 41 concerts

ABBA: THE TOUR
USA, Canada, France,
West Germany,
Netherlands, Ireland,
UK, Denmark
(13 September–15
November)

SUPER TROUPERS

Despite an antipathy to touring, ABBA were conscientious and meticulous about designing, staging and rehearsing their shows. Their aim was to replicate as precisely as possible the sound of their records on stage. They used backing tracks and hired extra musicians and backing singers – whatever it took to build the Tretow Wall of Sound. At the same time, they presented their audience with glamour and spectacle: extravagant props, specially commissioned costumes, choreography, lights, bubbles and fireworks. They were not interested in creating an edgy, spontaneous atmosphere or unleashing any Dionysiac rock 'n' roll urges. Many critics at the time thought their shows cold, clinical and emotionless: all glitter and no soul. Their fans did not agree.

13 SESSION MUSICIANS

AMPS:

20,000W stereo PA system

LIGHTING:

120,000W lighting system
2x Super Trouper spotlights

Made by Strong Lighting, a Super Trouper is a follow spotlight, with a brilliant white light that separates the performer from the ambient stage lighting.

2x guitarists
(Lasse Wellander,
Finn Sjöberg)

2x keyboard players
(Anders Eljas,
Wojciech Ernest)

1x drummer
(Ola Brunkert)

1x percussionist
(Malando Gassama)

1x bass guitarist
(Rutger
Gunnarsson)

3x backing singers
(Lena Andersson, Lena-
Maria Gårdenäs-Lawton,
Maritza Horn)

**2x saxophone/
flute players**
(Ulf Andersson,
Lars O. Karlsson)

and...
1x actor
(Francis
Matthews, who
narrated the
mini-musical
section, *The
Girl with the
Golden Hair*)

**17-piece string
section**
(The Australian
Musician's
Union insisted
there were as
many local
as touring
musicians.)

SFX:

Finale fireworks

71

THE WIZARDS OF OZ

ABBA were huge in Australia. In 1975, the country fell truly, madly, deeply in love with them, an intense two-year affair that made a lasting impact, especially on the young. In March 1976, the group made a promotional visit to capitalize on the success of a string of hit singles, and with Australian broadcasting company Network 9, made a TV film, *The Best of ABBA*. It featured their latest release, 'Fernando', which a besotted public took to number one and kept there for months. When the band returned for a concert tour the following year, full-on ecstatic ABBA-mania broke out. They played nine concerts across four cities to packed venues, then they left and the spell was broken.

THE NUMBER ONES

From October 1975 to December 1976, ABBA topped the Australian charts for 42 weeks over a 63-week period, sometimes consecutively.

THE TOUR 1977

PERTH

9–13 March:
5 concerts,
capacity
8,000

ADELAIDE

1 concert,
capacity
21,000

(10,000
more outside)

**13 October
1975**

**20 December
1976**

■ **13–27 Oct 1975:
'I Do, I Do, I Do'**

■ **3 Nov 1975–
5 Jan 1976:
'Mamma Mia'**

■ **12 Jan 1976:
'SOS'**

□ **5 Apr–5 July 1976:
'Fernando'**

□ **6 Sept–25 Oct 1976:
'Dancing Queen'**

□ **15 Nov–20 Dec 1976:
'Money, Money, Money'**

In 1976, the TV show *The Best of ABBA* on Network 9 was watched by 58% of the Australian viewing public, more than had watched the Moon landing in 1969.

145,000 TICKETS SOLD

MELBOURNE

5–7 March
3 concerts,
capacity
14,000

(16,000 more
outside at
first concert)

SYDNEY

3–4 March
2 concerts,
capacity
20,000

CAN YOU HEAR THE DRUMS?

ABBA's best-selling single was 'Fernando', which knocked Queen's 'Bohemian Rhapsody' off the top spot, and stayed there for 14 consecutive weeks, beating the record of 13 weeks set by The Beatles' 'Hey Jude' (1968).

1 IN 3

**Australian households
owned an ABBA record.**

ABBA: THE MOVIES

ABBA wanted their fans to see them performing, but also wanted to maintain control over how they were seen. So they hired fledgling director Lasse Hallström to make short films – promo clips – of every single they made, to send out to TV stations all over the world. They wanted plain, unpretentious and straightforward presentations of their songs, made on a modest budget and an even more modest schedule. Limitation can do wonders for creativity. Hallström used tight close-ups, live locations and ingenious positioning, and cut his film to the beat of the music, creating a distinct visual signature. He and ABBA were ahead of the game: MTV would not launch until 1981, the year before the band split.

Although ABBA were not the first to make promotional videos, theirs set a style that many would follow. Hallström shot one, or even two, a day on 16mm film in a cinéma-vérité style. In videos like 'Mamma Mia', he used extreme close-ups and riffed on the 'two couples' theme by using different combinations of face-on and profile, switching them to the beat.

Hallström worked with ABBA from 1974 ('Waterloo'), until 1982 ('Head over Heels'), directing 31 out of the 38 videos they made.

Hallström went on to become a Hollywood director, whose films include:

What's Eating Gilbert Grape? (1993)

The Cider House Rules (1999)

Chocolat (2000)

ABBA: The Movie was Hallström's first feature film, a drama-documentary made while the band was in Australia in 1977. Shot on 35mm with a running time of 97 minutes, it follows a hapless radio DJ trying to get an interview with ABBA and following them to every venue on the tour. It is now a cult classic.

1. Instruments in close-up
2. Group performing with sparse backdrop
3. Split into pairs
4. Cut between dynamic profiles

INFLUENCES

Where did ABBA find their unique sound? Early musical influences came at them through Swedish radio, with its determinedly fair-minded mix of traditional Scandinavian folk, buttoned-down Americana and European light classics. When the Sixties hit, their ears were opened to a different beat, but rather than rebel against their formative traditions, they married them together with rock 'n' roll rhythms filtered through veils of pop. It's hard to pin down any undiluted blues influences, but you could argue that as Scandinavians they were no strangers to existential melancholy; they had their own blues, it just played out to a different rhythm.

SWEDISH FOLK SONGS

GLAM ROCK

GERMAN MARCHING BANDS

MOTOWN

PHIL SPECTOR

SCHLAGER MUSIC

LATIN MUSIC

NORWEGIAN FOLK SONGS

BRILL BUILDING SONGWRITERS

THE BEACH BOYS

BUBBLEGUM POP

ITALIAN ARIAS

JAZZ

FRENCH CHANSONS

COUNTRY ROCK

AMERICAN FOLK

AMERICAN DISCO

AUSTRIAN OPERETTA

AMERICAN FEMALE SINGERS

LIGHT CLASSICAL

● **Childhood influences**

● **Songwriting influences**

THE BEATLES

ABBA

04
LEGACY

"WE TOOK A BREAK IN '82,
AND IT WAS MEANT
TO BE A BREAK...

IT'S STILL A BREAK AND WILL REMAIN SO. YOU'LL NEVER SEE US ON STAGE AGAIN."

—Björn Ulvaeus, *Billboard*, 2014

BJÖRN AGAIN AND AGAIN!

When ABBA dismantled themselves in 1982, they left a void. All four members moved on to new projects, and although there was no categorical denial of ever working together again, there was no categorical promise that they would. Stig Anderson's maverick attitude to tax matters caused huge financial problems that destroyed the band's relationship with him and nearly ruined them. Their back catalogue was licensed to budget labels for peanuts. ABBA seemed dead in the water. Then, in 1988, four young Australians created an affectionately parodic tribute show: Björn Again. Audiences loved it, and Björn and Benny, slightly bemused, gave it their blessing. Its success kickstarted the ABBA revival, inspiring the formation of more tribute acts and encouraging the real ABBA to release *Abba Gold* in 1992.

Björn Again has been through many line-ups, with only its founder directors, Rod Stephen and John Tyrrell, remaining a constant. The show is regularly refreshed with choreography, interactive audience participation, new setlists and rap. It is widely considered to be the best ABBA tribute act, indeed the best tribute act of all time.

FOUNDED: MELBOURNE | 1988

FOUNDERS:

Rod Stephen, John Tyrrell

ORIGINAL MEMBERS:

Björn Volvo-us
(Gavin Charles)
Agnetha Falstart
(Janette Stuart)
Frida Longstokin
(Dorina Morelli)
Benny Anderwear
(Peter Ryan)

Rutger Sonnofagun
(modelled on ABBA's
bassist Rutger Gunnarson)
Ola Drumkitt
(modelled on ABBA's
drummer Ola Brunkert)

LONGEVITY:

ABBA ▐▐▐▐▐▐▐ **10 YEARS**

Björn Again ▐▐▐▐▐▐▐▐▐▐▐▐▐▐▐▐▐▐ **32 YEARS**
and counting!

"BJÖRN AGAIN ARE THE CLOSEST YOU CAN GET TO SEEING ABBA. ABBA WILL NEVER RE-FORM!"

—Benny Andersson, 1999

SHOWS:

7,000

COUNTRIES PLAYED:

100

TOP GIGS:

1992:
Reading Festival,
opening for Nirvana
at Kurt Cobain's
request

1998:
Royal Albert
Hall, London

2019:
Glastonbury
Festival,
Pyramid Stage

BOOKED BY:
Russell Crowe
Bill Gates
Vladimir Putin

SINGLES:

ALBUMS:

COVERING ABBA

In the 1970s, when ABBA were in their pomp, it became a bit of a cliché for the in-crowd to mock them for their cheesy Europop sensibility, perma-smiles, ridiculous stagewear, lack of edge and apparently artless bubblegum aesthetic. Once they had stopped performing, however, and all the uncool surface dressing was stripped away, their songs were revealed as the solid, superbly engineered pieces of work they really are. The craft in them was especially appreciated by musicians of all genres, who started to cover them, led by British synth-pop duo Erasure with their 1992 EP *Abba-esque*. The love that had dared not speak its name, now came right out and sang it...

ABBA have been covered by artists in almost every genre: the most startling of which is heavy metal. Metal bands love ABBA songs, effortlessly aligning themselves with the fatalistic blend of gloom and glitter, upbeat tunes and downer lyrics, anthemic choruses and operatic chords. Indie and punk musicians also appreciate ABBA's contradictory tensions.

BA

- A cappella
- Alt country
- Alt rock
- Big band
- Bluegrass
- Choral
- Divas
- Easy listening
- Electro-pop
- Folk
- Funk
- Heavy metal
- Hindi-pop
- Indie
- Instrumental
- Jazz
- Light classical
- Operatic
- Punk
- Rock
- Synth-pop

MAMMA MIA!

This juggernaut of a jukebox musical (and subsequent movies) shot ABBA back into the world's consciousness, reinvigorated their back catalogue and turbocharged their already astronomical record sales. Yet it had taken theatrical impresario Judy Craymer over a decade to persuade Björn and Benny to let her develop a story from their songs. They had met in 1983 while working on *Chess* (the Tim Rice musical about Cold War grand masters) and Craymer had been impressed with 'The Winner Takes it All', a song that packs a huge narrative punch. When the ABBA team finally agreed, she commissioned playwright Catherine Johnson to write the book and Phyllida Lloyd to direct. The resultant musical opened in London's West End in 1999 and was an instant smash. It's still going strong, and is now a global hit. The movie version (2008) and its sequel (2018) are box-office gold. The winner did indeed take it all.

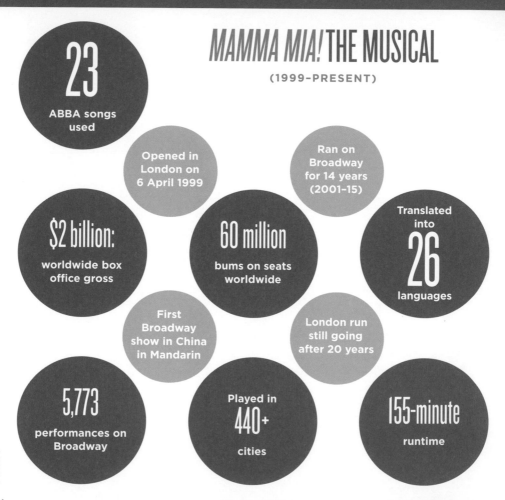

MAMMA MIA! THE MUSICAL

(1999–PRESENT)

23
ABBA songs used

Opened in London on 6 April 1999

Ran on Broadway for 14 years (2001–15)

$2 billion:
worldwide box office gross

60 million
bums on seats worldwide

Translated into **26** languages

First Broadway show in China in Mandarin

London run still going after 20 years

5,773
performances on Broadway

Played in **440+** cities

155-minute
runtime

BASIC PLOT

MOTHER

DAUGHTER

FATHER

MAMMA MIA! THE MOVIE

(2008)

21 ABBA songs used

Premiered in London on 30 June 2008

The UK's highest-grossing movie of all time

1 in 4 households in the UK owns the DVD

Took **$30 million** on first day of DVD release in US

$615 million: worldwide box office gross

Best-selling DVD of all time in Sweden

Won MTV Best Musical Award in 2009

108-minute runtime

5 million DVDs sold in the UK

$52 million budget

MONEY, MONEY, MONEY

ABBA have become rather un-Swedishly super-rich (being super-rich is not considered *lagom*, see page 38). At one point, they even got paid in oil credits. Although it's been almost 40 years since they performed together, and all of them have been doing other things, the money from their decade at the top has kept rolling in at an even faster rate. An early decision, inspired by Lennon and McCartney, to write their own songs, and a professional perfectionism that wouldn't let an inferior product out of the studio, means that the ABBA product is a musical blue chip that will constantly yield rewards: a sound investment.

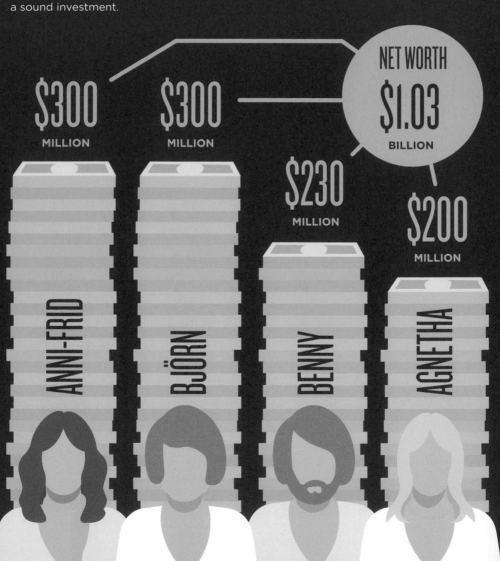

$300 MILLION — ANNI-FRID

$300 MILLION — BJÖRN

$230 MILLION — BENNY

$200 MILLION — AGNETHA

NET WORTH $1.03 BILLION

HOW MANY ABBAS IN 1 VOLVO?

$35.35
BILLION

If ABBA is worth $1 billion and Volvo is worth $35.53 billion you would need:
35 and a half ABBAs to make one Volvo.

HOW MANY ABBAS IN 1 IKEA?

$58.7
BILLION

If IKEA is worth $58.7 billion you would need:
59 ABBAs to make one IKEA.

AND McCARTNEY?

$1.2
BILLION

Paul McCartney's net worth is $1.2 billion, slightly more than ABBA's.

MAMMA MIA!

One source of ABBA riches is *Mamma Mia!* in its different forms: **$4 billion** grossed by *Mamma Mia!* the musical after launching in 1999; **$615.7 million** taken at box office by *Mamma Mia!* the movie (2008).

WHAT BENNY AND BJÖRN DID NEXT

Benny and Björn were the really solid couple in the band, and they are still living happily ever after in a musical partnership. Both turned to new projects and new marriage partners almost embarrassingly quickly after ABBA ran out of steam in 1982. They continued producing music, collaborating on songs and musicals, and winning awards together. Outside the musical partnership, Björn took care of business, and Benny took care of the music, and they still do. Björn is busy masterminding the maximization of the *Mamma Mia!* juggernaut while campaigning for a cashless society. When not touring Sweden with his orchestra, Benny mellows out with his string of racehorses.

5 ALBUMS

1981 DIVORCES FROM ANNI-FRID

MARRIES TV PRESENTER MONA NÖRKLIT

1990 WRITES 'LASSIE', NO. 1 HIT FOR ALL-GIRL BAND, AINBUSK

#1

2012 WRITES *PALME*, SCORE FOR DOCUMENTARY ON ASSASSINATED PRIME MINISTER OLOF PALME

2001 FORMS 16-PIECE BAND, BAO (BENNY ANDERSSONS ORKESTER)

1981 DIVORCES FROM AGNETHA

MARRIES MUSIC JOURNALIST LENA KÄLLERSJÖ

1984
MOVES TO ENGLAND TO DEVELOP IT COMPANY WITH BROTHER

2013
CAMPAIGNS FOR CASHLESS SOCIETY

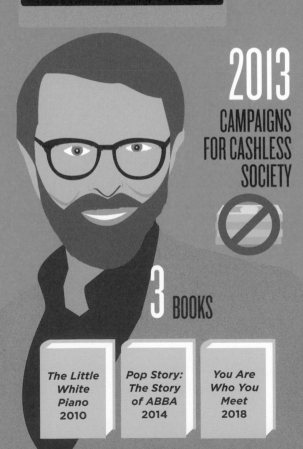

3 BOOKS

The Little White Piano 2010

Pop Story: The Story of ABBA 2014

You Are Who You Meet 2018

WHAT THEY DID TOGETHER

1984	Write *Chess* with Sir Tim Rice, a musical about Cold War passion
1992 1999	Arrange music, re-record songs and act as executive producers for *Mamma Mia!* the musical
1995 1999	Write *Kristina Från Duvemala*, a musical based on *The Emigrants* by Vilhelm Moberg
2001	Receive Lifetime Achievement Award from Swedish Music Publishers Association
2001	Receive International Ivor Novello Award for Songwriting
2008	Awarded Music Export Prize from Swedish Government
2010	ABBA is inducted into Hall of Fame by Robin and Barry Gibb
2013	Write 'We Write the Story', the anthem for the 2013 Eurovision Song Contest
2020	Announce that new ABBA songs will be released, almost 30 years after band dissolved

WHAT AGNETHA AND ANNI-FRID DID NEXT

When the music stopped, the two As, always the literal outsiders, spun away from the group and traced remarkably similar, but entirely separate, post-ABBA trajectories. Both reinvigorated their solo careers with initial success; both worked with international record producers to escape the ABBA sound; both won prestigious accolades; both dabbled in movies; both took long breaks from the music business; both endured family tragedies. Agnetha, the shy, small-town, sweet-voiced princess who hated the limelight, now lives in happy seclusion with her family. Anni-Frid, the outsider who loved performing, is now a real-life princess with a life on the international stage.

5 ALBUMS

1982 STARS IN ROM-COM, *RASKENSTAM*

1986 RELEASES 'THE WAY YOU ARE', DUET WITH OLA KAKANSSON **#1**

1982 RELEASES 'NEVER AGAIN', DUET WITH TOMAS LEDIN **#5**

1988–2004 CAREER BREAK

2013 SINGS LIVE FOR FIRST TIME IN 25 YEARS AT BBC CHILDREN IN NEED CONCERT

3 ALBUMS

1984
APPEARS IN, COMEDY SKETCH FILM, *JOKERFEJS*

1987
SINGS ON BENNY'S SOLO ALBUM, *KLINGA MINA KLOCKOR*

2004
GUESTS ON JON LORD (DEEP PURPLE) ALBUM, *BEYOND THE NOTES*

1988–1996 CAREER BREAK

WHAT HAPPENED IN THEIR PERSONAL LIVES

1986 Anni-Frid moves to Switzerland

1990 Agnetha marries surgeon Tomas Sonnenfeld

1992 Anni-Frid marries Prince Heinrich Ruzzo Reuss von Plauen

1993 Agnetha divorces

1994 Agnetha's mother commits suicide

1995 Agnetha's father dies

1997 Agnetha begins relationship with Dutchman Gert van der Graaf

1998 Anni-Frid's daughter Lise-Lotte is killed in a road accident

1999 Anni-Frid's husband Prince Heinrich dies of cancer

2000 Agnetha's ex-boyfriend, Van der Graaf, is deported for stalking her

2008 Anni-Frid shares home with Henry Smith, Fifth Earl of Hambledon

BIOGRAPHIES

Rutger Gunnarsson (1946–2015)
Bassist, guitarist and arranger, Gunnarsson was the main bass player on all ABBA records, and toured with them. Working alongside Benny and Michael Tretow, he was not just a session musician, but created his own bass lines and musical parts.

Polar Music Prize (founded 1989)
Set up by Stig Anderson on behalf of Polar Music, this is an annual prize of 1 million Swedish kroner awarded in two categories, popular and classical music. The first recipients were Paul McCartney and the Baltic States.

Rune Söderqvist (1935–2014)
Graphic designer, well established in advertising before finding wider fame as creator of the ABBA logo and shaper of their brand. He designed all their album sleeves and, with Owe Sandström, the stage sets for the 1977 and 1979 tours.

Michael B. Tretow (b. 1944)
Sound engineer, producer, musician and composer. The perfectionist technician to Benny Andersson's musical architect, Tretow worked with all four members before, during and after the ABBA years, and continued to update their catalogue until 2015.

Christina Grönvall (b. 1945)
Benny's first partner. They met in 1962 as teenagers in a band (she was the singer), got engaged, and produced two children before splitting in 1966. Their relationship was kept secret to protect Benny's rock god status in the Hep Stars.

Ola Brunkert (1946–2008)
ABBA's main drummer throughout the 1970s. He played on every album, toured with their stage shows and played at the fateful Eurovision Song Contest in 1974. He died as a result of a bizarre glass-related accident at his home in Mallorca.

**Ragnar Fredriksson
(b. 1941)**
Anni-Frid's first husband. He was the trombonist, she the 16-year-old singer in the Bengt Sandlund Big Band. They formed the Anni-Frid Four, married and produced two children. They divorced amicably in 1970.

**Lars
Sven 'Lasse'
Hallström
(b. 1946)**
Stockholm-born film-maker only one year into his career when chosen by ABBA to make their groundbreaking videos. A decade later, Hallström was in Hollywood making movies including *My Life as a Dog* (1985) and *Chocolat* (2000).

**Stig
Eric Leopold
Anderson
(1931–97)**
Music biz entrepreneur, songwriter and co-founder of Polar Music. He pounced on the foursome's potential, used canny promotion to propel them to the top, but nearly ruined it all with cavalier business methods. Died after a struggle with alcohol.

**Alfred
Haase
(1919–2009)**
Anni-Frid's German father. Posted with the Wehrmacht to Norway in 1943, he had a wartime love affair with Synni Lyngstad. He left in 1945, seven months before Anni-Frid was born, and knew nothing of her existence. They met in 1977.

**Prince
Heinrich Ruzzo
Reuss von Plauen
(1950–99)**
Anni-Frid's third husband. A Swiss prince with a Swedish mother, he worked in Stockholm as an architect and was good friends with King Carl Gustav XVI. The pair met in 1986 and married in 1992. He died from lymphoma.

**Karl Owe
Sandström
(b. 1944)**
Clothes designer, teacher, TV presenter and animal expert. With Lars Wigenius, his partner in Artist Dressing, he designed over 500 of ABBA's glam rock costumes and their stage sets. He was key to creating ABBA's image.

● **Personal and family**

● **The ABBA image team**

● **Musicians**

● **Legacy**

INDEX